When Faith Is All You Have

A Study of Hebrews 11

RUTH E. VAN REKEN

FISHERMAN
BIBLE STUDY SERIES

WHEN FAITH IS ALL YOU HAVE

Trade Paperback ISBN 978-0-87788-027-1

eBook ISBN 978-0-307-55259-4

Published in the United States by WaterBrook, an imprint of the Crown Publishing Group, a division of Penguin Random House LLC, New York.

Printed in the United States of America

2017

15 14 13

*This book is dedicated with love and thanks
to those who taught me firsthand, from my earliest days on,
what it means to walk by faith—my father and mother,
Charles and Betty Frame.*

Contents

Acknowledgments

I thank God for the incredible examples of faith-filled lives he has granted me through my grandmother Varnell; my wonderful aunts and uncles, including the aunts who helped raise me at various points when my parents were overseas as missionaries—Edna Mae Dumper, Lois Ruth Balzer, and Ellen Jennette Gottlieb; and last, but certainly not least, my parents-in-law, Everett and Rose Van Reken. My life has been made rich indeed from all I have learned from each of them.

And I thank my editor, Mary Horner Collins, for her outstanding partnership in helping put some of what I have learned about living by faith into a form others can use. Without her and the ongoing help of Elisa Fryling Stanford and Jennifer Lonas, this study would not be. I also thank the WaterBrook design team for their excellent work on the cover.

How to Use This Studyguide

F isherman studyguides are based on the inductive approach to Bible study. Inductive study is discovery study; we discover what the Bible says as we ask questions about its content and search for answers. This is quite different from the process in which a teacher *tells* a group *about* the Bible— what it means and what to do about it. In inductive study, God speaks directly to each of us through his Word.

A group functions best when a leader keeps the discussion on target, but the leader is neither the teacher nor the "answer person." A leader's responsibility is to *ask*—not *tell*. The answers come from the text itself as group members examine, discuss, and think together about the passage.

There are four kinds of questions in each study. The first is an *approach question*. Asked and answered before the Bible passage is read, this question breaks the ice and helps you start thinking about the topic of the Bible study. It begins to reveal where thoughts and feelings need to be transformed by Scripture.

Some of the earlier questions in each study are *observation questions*—who, what, where, when, and how—designed to help you learn some basic facts about the passage of Scripture.

Once you know what the Bible says, you need to ask, *What does it mean?* These *interpretation questions* help you discover the writer's basic message.

Next come *application questions*, which ask, *What does it mean to me?* They challenge you to live out the Scripture's life-transforming message.

Fisherman studyguides provide spaces between questions for jotting down responses as well as any related questions you would like to raise in the group. Each group member should have a copy of the studyguide and may take a turn in leading the group.

A group should use any accurate, modern translation of the Bible such as the *New International Version*, the *New American Standard Bible*, the *New Living Translation*, the *New Revised Standard Version*, the *New Jerusalem Bible*, or the *Good News Bible*. (Other translations or paraphrases of the Bible may be referred to when additional help is needed.) Bible commentaries should not be brought to a Bible study because they tend to dampen discussion and keep people from thinking for themselves.

Suggestions for Group Leaders

1. Thoroughly read and study the Bible passage before the meeting. Get a firm grasp on its themes and begin applying its teachings for yourself. Pray that the Holy Spirit will "guide you into all truth" (John 16:13) so that your leadership will guide others.

2. If any of the studyguide's questions seem ambiguous or unnatural to you, rephrase them, feeling free to add others that seem necessary to bring out the meaning of a verse.

3. Begin (and end) the study promptly. Start by asking someone to pray that every participant will both understand the passage and be open to its transforming power. Remember, the Holy Spirit is the teacher, not you!

4. Ask for volunteers to read the passages aloud.

5. As you ask the studyguide's questions in sequence, encourage everyone to participate in the discussion. If some are silent, try gently suggesting, "Let's have an answer from someone who hasn't spoken up yet."

6. If a question comes up that you can't answer, don't be afraid to admit that you're baffled. Assign the topic as a research project for someone to report on next week, or say, "I'll do some studying and let you know what I find out."

7. Keep the discussion moving, but be sure it stays focused. Though a certain number of tangents are inevitable, you'll want to quickly bring the discussion back to the topic at hand. Also, learn to pace the discussion so that you finish the lesson in the time allotted.

8. Don't be afraid of silences; some questions take time to answer, and some people need time to gather courage to speak. If silence persists, rephrase your question, but resist the temptation to answer it yourself.

9. If someone comes up with an answer that is clearly illogical or unbiblical, ask for further clarification: "What verse suggests that to you?"

10. Discourage overuse of cross references. Learn all you can from the passage at hand, while selectively incorporating a few important references suggested in the studyguide.

11. Some questions are marked with a *⌀*. This indicates that further information is available in the Leader's Notes at the back of the guide.

12. For further information on getting a new Bible study group started and keeping it functioning effectively, read *You Can Start a Bible Study Group* by Gladys Hunt and *Pilgrims in Progress: Growing Through Groups* by Jim and Carol Plueddemann. (Both books are available from Shaw Books).

SUGGESTIONS FOR GROUP MEMBERS

1. Learn and apply the following ground rules for effective Bible study. (If new members join the group later, review these guidelines with the whole group.)
2. Remember that your goal is to learn all that you can *from the Bible passage being studied.* Let it speak for itself without using Bible commentaries or other Bible passages. There is more than enough in each assigned passage to keep your group productively occupied for one session. Sticking to the passage saves the group from insecurity ("I don't have the right reference books—or the time to read anything else.") and confusion ("Where did *that* come from? I thought we were studying _____.").
3. Avoid the temptation to bring up those fascinating tangents that don't really grow out of the passage you are discussing. If the topic is of common interest, you can bring it up later in informal conversation after the study. Meanwhile, help one another stick to the subject.
4. Encourage one another to participate. People remember best what they discover and verbalize for

themselves. Some people are naturally shy, while others may be afraid of making a mistake. If your discussion is free and friendly and you show real interest in what other group members think and feel, the quieter ones will be more likely to speak up. Remember, the more people involved in a discussion, the richer it will be.

5. Guard yourself from answering too many questions or talking too much. Give others a chance to share their ideas. If you are one who participates easily, discipline yourself by counting to ten before you open your mouth.

6. Make personal, honest applications and commit yourself to letting God's Word change you.

Introduction

A few years ago I had a major crisis of faith. For nine years my husband and I worked in Liberia. Shortly after we returned to the United States, civil war ravaged that country and the people we had come to love. The hospital and medical school my husband had worked in were looted and closed. Many people in whom we'd invested our lives died in the war or were forced to live as refugees in other countries. It seemed that everything we had tried so hard to build was now destroyed.

In the middle of this situation, I began reading Hebrews 11 and came to verse 6: "Without faith it is impossible to please God, because anyone who comes to him must believe that he exists and that he rewards those who earnestly seek him." And my faith battle began.

Hadn't I come to God time and again on behalf of Liberia and my friends caught up in the war? But the war had only gotten worse, people kept dying, more destruction took place. Nothing seemed to be as it should be if these verses were true. Could it be that the God I thought worthy enough to give my whole life to serve was just a joke? If not, what was this "faith" God asked of me?

Those moments of wrestling with God gave birth to this study. I realized that God put each of the people listed in Hebrews 11 in his illustrious hall of faith because somehow, in spite of widely differing circumstances, they had successfully lived "by faith." I wanted to know their secret.

Was faith a feeling they learned or a gift they received?

Was it primarily something they believed or something they did?

Did faith come through an event or as a process?

Could it be all of the above—or none of the above?

I pray that this study will help you discover the answers to these questions for yourself. Since Hebrews 11 assumes a knowledge of the biblical events and people listed in this faith chapter, we will explore the stories of some of these biblical characters in the Old Testament, looking for that common thread of faith in their lives. Each study also gives the reference for the complete scriptural account of the person whose story you are studying. Whenever possible, take time to read the entire story before you begin to answer the questions. This overview will help put the shorter vignettes of each lesson in context and will hopefully lead you to deeper discoveries of this life-changing topic of what it means to live by faith—a faith that keeps you hanging on and believing God, no matter what.

What Is Faith?

HEBREWS 10:32–11:6; GENESIS 4:1-8; 5:21-24

Faith is an odd word. We think we know what it means until we try to describe it. People use it in many ways: "Keep the faith, sister." "Just have faith." But what does it mean? Is it simply a slogan? an idea we believe in? the right doctrine? a concept?

The Bible uses the word *faith* more than 230 times. Obviously, it's an important topic. We begin our study on living by faith with a look at the word itself.

1. Is *faith* the same as *belief*? If so, how are they the same? If not, how are they different?

Read Hebrews 11:1-6.

2. What is the writer's definition of *faith* (verse 1)?

How is this definition similar to or different from your answer in question 1?

3. How does the writer illustrate his definition of *faith* (verse 3)?

Read Hebrews 10:32-39.

✐ 4. Describe the situation these Hebrew Christians faced and their reactions to it (verses 32-34).

5. What did the writer admonish them to do (verses 35-39)?

How does this relate to his definition of *faith* in Hebrews 11:1?

READ HEBREWS 11:4 AND GENESIS 4:1-8.

6. How did God respond to both brothers and their offerings?

ᔮ 7. Compare Abel's story with the definition of *faith* in Hebrews 11:1. What do you think qualified him to be included in the list of those who lived "by faith"?

READ HEBREWS 11:5 AND GENESIS 5:21-24.

8. List everything these scriptures tell us about Enoch.

🖉 9. Think about how you would describe someone you know and what important details you might mention. Why do you think God chose to list only these brief details about Enoch through the writers of Hebrews and Genesis?

🖉 10. Read Hebrews 11:6 again. Why do you think we cannot please God without faith?

In whom or what should our faith be?

11.   How does this kind of faith change our lives? Why?

FAITH INTO LIFE

Ask God to show you any area where your faith is faltering because what you *see* seems more real than what you *don't* see. Then ask him to help you focus on who he is, not just on what he is or is not doing at the moment.

When Faith Makes You Look Like a Fool

SELECTIONS FROM GENESIS 5–8; HEBREWS 11:7
(COMPLETE STORY: GENESIS 5–9)

In addition to the clear instructions God gives in his Word, he also speaks to us through his Holy Spirit. Sometimes the specific things we believe God asks us to do through that soft inner voice of the Spirit can make little human sense. Yet, by faith we seek to be obedient to God and to follow where he leads, presuming that one day he will prove we heard him right. But sometimes what we expect or believe he has promised us (and what we've told others!) doesn't seem to be happening. Those are hard moments indeed. At such times it's easy to wonder, *Did God forget? Has he hung me out to dry in front of the whole world? Am I just plain wrong in believing I heard him?*

Noah may have had similar moments of doubt in the long years between God's call and the day the rains began. As we explore Noah's story of faith, we'll find clues to what kept him obeying God, no matter how foolish his assignment seemed.

1. Can you think of a time you believed you heard God tell you something specific (e.g., to change jobs, to reach out to someone, to wait for a loved one's healing), but as you obeyed, the outcome was different from what you expected? How did you feel? What did you do?

READ GENESIS 5:21-32.

2. What facts do we learn about Noah in this passage?

🖉 3. Review what you learned about Noah's great-grandfather Enoch in the first study (verses 21-24; see also Hebrews 11:5). How might Noah's lineage have influenced his life?

READ GENESIS 6:5–7:5.

 4. What does 6:5-7 tell us about the state of the world in Noah's day?

What do these verses tell us about God?

5. Given all of these facts about the world and its people, how do you imagine each of the following groups responded when Noah began to build the ark?

his friends

the larger community

his family

✗ 6. God spoke to Noah in 6:13. How do you know
       Noah heard God (verse 22)?

       What does such a response have to do with living
       by faith?

   7. Note the seemingly impossible, almost crazy instruc-
       tions God gave Noah in 7:1-5. Again, how did Noah
       respond?

       How do you think you might have responded to the
       same instructions?

READ GENESIS 8:15-22.

8. Noah and his entourage had been in the ark for more than one year. In what way do Noah's actions upon coming out of the ark reflect faith?

READ HEBREWS 11:7.

9. This verse describes Noah from God's perspective. What reason for Noah's obedience is given here?

✐ 10. How does living "in holy fear" shed light on what it means to live by faith?

✐ 11. What was the end result of Noah's faith?

FAITH INTO LIFE

Has God ever asked you to do something so "foolish" that you dismissed his promptings? Dare to ask God for a faith like Noah's that will enable you to follow wherever and however he leads you. You may be amazed at what happens!

When Faith Doesn't See the Promise Fulfilled

GENESIS 12:1-5; HEBREWS 11:8-19
(COMPLETE STORY: GENESIS 12:1–25:11)

A s a child I learned countless Bible promises that said if I had faith, God would grant my requests—even to the point of moving the mountain towering outside the window of my first-grade classroom. No matter how earnestly I believed or prayed, however, I never saw that mountain move.

What do we do when it seems as if God is not doing what he said he would do? Sometimes I excuse God by faulting my faith. As a child I took the blame for that unmovable mountain: "Well, I must not have *really* believed it would move, or God would have done what I asked, since that's what he promised." At other times I give God an excuse: "Well, if God didn't move the mountain this time, he must be planning something really special for it in the future."

What's the problem when we don't see God doing what he has promised? Is it his promises? our faith? sin? Surely Abraham had such questions as he waited for the fulfillment of promises God had made to him. In this lesson we see how Abraham handled waiting.

1. When someone makes a promise, what factors cause us to believe—or not believe—that person?

READ GENESIS 12:1-5.

2. What did God tell Abram to do (verse 1)?

3. What two things did God promise if Abram obeyed him (verse 2)?

In this initial moment, how do you think Abram expected God to fulfill those promises?

☞ 4. Why do you think Abram took Lot with him as he journeyed to this unknown place, even though God told him to leave his father's household?

5. God repeated his promise to Abram four more times. Read each passage on the following page, noting what is the same in each promise and what is different or progressively added in each one. Read the surrounding verses and make a guess as to why this might have been a key time for such a renewal.

☞ 6. How many years had passed from the first promise to the fifth promise? (See Genesis 12:4 and Genesis 17:1 for some hints.)

Scripture Reference	Promises Identical to Original Promise	Clarification of or Additions to the Original Promise	Circumstances Surrounding the Promise
Genesis 12:1-3 (original promise)	(original details)	(none)	
Genesis 13:14-17			
Genesis 15:1-6			
Genesis 17:3-8,15-16			
Genesis 22:15-18			

Why do you think God didn't give all the details at the beginning?

READ HEBREWS 11:8-19.

7. List each thing Abraham did "by faith."

What did Abraham have to believe before he could take each of these actions?

🖉 8. Verses 17-19 summarize the story recorded in Genesis 22:1-18. In these verses we read of Abraham's willingness to sacrifice his son, Isaac. What made it possible for Abraham to trust

God to the point of being willing to sacrifice
his only son?

9. Verse 13 says that those who had been living by
    faith (verses 4-11) never lived to see the complete
    fulfillment of God's promises to them. What prom-
    ises did Abraham live to see? Which ones did he
    not see?

10. Why could all these people—including Abraham—
    continue living by faith even though they never
    received all that God had promised?

11. As you reflect on Abraham's life, what challenges or
    encourages your faith most?

FAITH INTO LIFE

Is there an area in your life in which you believe God has made a promise, but it remains unfulfilled? Write it down. Take time to let God comfort you when there is still no sign of an answer to the promises you long to see fulfilled. Be honest with him and ask him for strength and wisdom to continue living by faith in this and other areas of your life.

STUDY 4

When Faith Seems Ordinary

SELECTIONS FROM GENESIS 25:19-28; 26:1-6;
27:1-40; HEBREWS 11:20
(COMPLETE STORY: GENESIS 21:1–28:9; 35:27-29)

As a child I sometimes regretted that I had such an ordinary life. My parents were missionaries who taught in an elementary school. Nothing too spectacular there. Each morning they set off on their educational endeavors. Each evening they came home to mark papers and prepare the next day's lessons. One routine day after another. But during mission conferences I'd hear amazing stories of what others were doing: preaching to crowds and seeing mass conversions or God's radical intervention in the face of demonic power. Why didn't those kinds of things ever happen to us?

How does God decide which story he will give each of us to live out? Why do some people seem to get the "big call," while others pass virtually unnoticed throughout their entire sojourns on this earth? Today we study a man whose life would have appeared remarkably mundane compared to the lives of those around him—just another person living with his family and servants in some tents on a plain. Nothing too impressive there. The surprise is how God looked at this ordinary life lived by real faith.

1. How would you rank your life on a scale of 1 to 10, where 1 is the most humdrum existence imaginable and 10 is the most interesting and exciting life possible? Explain your answer.

Genesis 25:19-28.

2. List everything you learn about Isaac and his life in this passage.

✐ 3. What sign of Isaac's faith do you see in verse 21?

How might his own life story have helped make such faith possible?

🖋 4. After Rebekah became pregnant, what did God tell her about her future offspring (verse 23)?

Why is this important?

READ GENESIS 26:1-6.

5. Describe any similarities and differences between God's promise to Isaac in verses 2-5 and his promise to Abraham in Genesis 12:1-3?

∂ 6. Why might God have chosen this time in Isaac's life to specifically spell out these promises to him?

∂ 7. How was Isaac's response an act of faith (verse 6)?

READ GENESIS 27:1-40.

8. Describe the four main characters of this story. How might you best describe the dynamics in this family?

∂ 9. Even though Isaac mistakenly blessed the wrong son, how do we see his faith in God's covenantal promises expressed in his words to Jacob (verses 27-29)?

10. How did Isaac handle this seemingly irreversible turn of events?

What does this tell you about him?

11. Though Isaac already seemed to be quite old when he blessed his sons, he didn't die until approximately twenty years later (see Genesis 35:27-29). Imagine Isaac's life during these ordinary intervening years. What might have been his greatest challenge to persevering in faith during this time?

READ HEBREWS 11:20.

12. What reason did the writer of Hebrews give for including Isaac in this hall of faith?

Why do you think Isaac's action was such a big
deal?

Faith into Life

List some of God's promises that you can hold on to this week
whether or not you see great events happening in your daily
life. Remember the importance of Isaac in God's story the next
time you begin to doubt his plan and promises for you.

When Faith Seems Absent

GENESIS 28:10-22; 32; 35:1-5; HEBREWS 11:21
(COMPLETE STORY: GENESIS 25:19-34;
28-35; 46-49)

T he first time I taught on Hebrews 11, I said to my class,
"I don't know why God put Jacob in this hall of faith.
He is such a cheat and scoundrel." My good friend Barb
Knuckles called me the next day, saying, "Ruth, where do you
get your idea of what human beings are supposed to be? You
begin with an image that they should be 100 percent perfect,
and if they're anything less, they're worthless. I think God
starts at a very different place with us. He begins at zero, for he
knows who we truly are. Then with every step we make in his
direction, he is cheering for us."

Barb, of course, was right. That's what grace is all about—
God pursuing us when we have no particular desire or incli-
nation to pursue him. And of all the people we are studying,
Jacob demonstrates more clearly than any other the mystery of
this grace.

1. Do you know anyone (maybe even you!) who, in running away from God, discovered he or she had run *into* him? Briefly explain.

From his earliest days Jacob connived and deceived to steal the birthright and blessing that rightfully belonged to his older brother, Esau. When Esau understandably wished to kill him, Jacob decided it was time to visit his Uncle Laban in a distant land. With the help of his mother, Jacob slipped away and began a long journey to his ancestral roots. He wasn't on a spiritual quest or an altruistic mission; he only wanted to save his skin. Yet it was on this most unlikely journey that he had his first encounter with God. We pick up his story there.

READ GENESIS 28:10-22.

2. Who initiated this special event on Jacob's journey?

⊘ 3. List the promises Jacob received during his dream
       (verses 13-15). What makes them particularly
       significant?

       Did Jacob deserve these promises? Why or why not?

4. Compare Jacob's vow in verses 20-22 with God's
    promises in verses 13-15. What does Jacob's
    response tell you about his faith at that point
    in time? Would you say his faith was conditional
    or unconditional? Why?

Read Genesis 32.

✐ 5. Whom did Jacob meet as he entered the land (verse 1)? Why might that have been important to Jacob?

6. What was Jacob's strategy for meeting up with his estranged brother?

What do you think motivated his actions?

7. What are the similarities and differences between Jacob's prayer in verses 9-12 and his initial prayer at Bethel (see Genesis 28:20-22)?

What, if anything, in that comparison indicates that Jacob's attitude or spirit had changed during the intervening years? Explain.

✐ 8.   Skim verses 22-32. This is where Jacob wrestled with God himself. Reflect on the following questions as you consider the full significance of such an encounter.

How did God overcome Jacob's resistance to him?

Why was it necessary to do this?

What happened to Jacob in the end?

9. Have there been similar times in your life when you've wrestled with God? If so, what has God done for you through such times?

READ GENESIS 35:1-5.

10. Why do you think God sent Jacob back to Bethel?

11. How had Jacob changed as a person and in his view of God from his first visit to Bethel to this visit?

What brought about that change?

READ HEBREWS 11:21.

✐ 12. In what two respects is Jacob described as living "by faith" at the end of his life?

Why is each action a reflection of faith?

FAITH INTO LIFE

Think about your journey with God. Have there been times he has pursued you, perhaps before you were aware of it? Have there been times when your faith has been absent or when you have resisted his working? Have you been left with any "limps" in your life? Remember, he who wrestled with Jacob is willing to let us wrestle with him as well. Talk with God about all of these matters. Give thanks where appropriate, repent if needed, submit if you're struggling, or accept what he has given to remind you of your dependence on him.

When Faith Trusts Enough to Forgive

GENESIS 37; 45:1-15; 50:15-26; HEBREWS 11:22
(COMPLETE STORY: GENESIS 37; 39–50)

W hat does it mean to forgive? Is it to sweep a wrong under the rug, pretending it never happened? Does it mean saying, "Oh, it doesn't matter," when you've been treated unfairly? A counselor friend of mine once told me that forgiveness is neither. She says that when Jesus forgives us, he looks our sin squarely in the face, acknowledges it is wrong, and forgives because it matters *so* much and there is no other way to restore things. Often true forgiveness means the wounded person bears the cost of what happened, while the perpetrator goes free.

When we look at the story of Joseph, we see an almost unbelievable example of a human being who had every reason to be vindictive, to retaliate, even to kill those who so unfairly sold him into a life of slavery and bondage. It is also here, however, where we see the amazing difference living by faith can make when it comes to forgiving those who have hurt us.

1. Whom is it easier to forgive: a family member or a stranger? Explain.

READ GENESIS 37.

✍ 2. What is happening in verses 1-4? How would you describe the inner workings of this family?

Whom would you consider most responsible for this state of affairs? Explain.

3. Why do you think Joseph told his family about his dreams instead of keeping them to himself?

How did his father and brothers respond (verses 5-11)? Do you blame them?

4. Skim through verses 12-36 again. Trace the trail of selfishness throughout this event. What do the brothers' actions reveal about what they placed their faith in?

 5. What effect did the brothers' deception have on their father?

6. Do you think the brothers accomplished what they wanted by getting rid of Joseph? Why or why not?

READ GENESIS 45:1-15.

 7. Years later a severe famine forced Joseph's brothers to go to Egypt to buy food, little knowing that Joseph was the ruler they were bowing before. In this moving reunion scene, how did Joseph's response compare with his brothers' response (verses 3-5)?

 8. What made it possible for Joseph to respond to his brothers the way he did?

How does his response relate to living by faith?

READ GENESIS 50:15-21.

9. How did Joseph's brothers react after their father's death?

Why do you think they behaved this way after all Joseph had already done for them?

10. How does Joseph's response to them encourage or challenge you in your faith journey?

READ GENESIS 50:22-26 AND HEBREWS 11:22.

11. When the time came for Joseph to die, what was his last request?

✐ 12. Of all the great things Joseph did during his life-
       time, why do you think the writer of Hebrews
       chose to mention this deathbed scene?

How does it express faith?

FAITH INTO LIFE

Hebrews 12:15 says, "See to it that no one misses the grace of
God and that no bitter root grows up to cause trouble and de-
file many." Are there areas in your life in which you struggle
with bitterness because someone has deeply hurt you or treated
you most unfairly? Consider again what made it possible for
Joseph to forgive his brothers. In a vertical line below, list the
letters of the person's name or the situation you're struggling
with. Next to each letter, write a characteristic of God that
begins with that letter. (For example: F–Faithful; E–Eternal;
A–All Knowing; R–Redeemer.) Does this reminder of who
God is change anything for you as you think on these things?

When Faith Receives an Impossible Call

EXODUS 3:1–4:20; HEBREWS 11:23-28
(COMPLETE STORY: EXODUS 1–14)

E ach description in Hebrews 11 is about people who lived by faith. Yet when we look at the complete accounts of their lives in the Old Testament, we see a wide variation in the details. For example, God asked Noah to risk appearing foolish before all his peers and carry out a difficult task. We never see one moment of questioning or disobedience. Instead, we read that "Noah did everything just as God commanded him" (Genesis 6:22). Noah's example of complete trust and obedience is a great encouragement to us.

In this study, however, we meet a person who encourages us in a different way. In fact, many of us probably relate to him more easily than to Noah. When God called, Moses argued and explained why he couldn't do what God was asking of him. But in the end God met him at the point of what little faith Moses could muster. Because of that, Moses lived to see amazing miracles he could never have imagined and to know the joy of being an ordinary person whom God used to do extraordinary things.

1. Have you ever been asked to do a task for which you didn't feel suited or gifted? How did you feel? What did you do?

READ EXODUS 3:1-10.

✐ 2. As the scene unfolds in verses 1-6, what was Moses doing when the Angel of the Lord appeared?

✐ 3. How do you account for the differences in Moses' responses in verses 4 and 6?

4. In verses 7-10, what do you learn about the heart of God? about the plight of the Israelites?

5. In verse 10, God told Moses his plan. What was it?

READ EXODUS 3:11–4:20.

6. In these verses we see an ongoing dialogue between Moses and God about the plan of deliverance for the Israelites. In the first column of the chart on the following page, list the reasons why Moses thought the plan wouldn't work. In the next column, list how God responded to each objection.

7. What was God's basic message to Moses in each answer? Does it seem to have been enough for Moses?

Scripture	Moses' Objections	Scripture	God's Reply
Exodus 3:11		Exodus 3:12	
Exodus 3:13		Exodus 3:14-22	
Exodus 4:1		Exodus 4:3-9	
Exodus 4:10		Exodus 4:11-12	
Exodus 4:13		Exodus 4:14-17	

8. If God were to say to you as he said to Moses, "What is that in your hand?" (4:2), what might your reply be? Explain.

Is the thing "in your hand" any more unlikely an instrument for God to use than Moses' staff? Explain.

↗ 9. In the end, what did Moses do (4:18-20)?

What does this tell you about Moses?

HEBREWS 11:23-28.

10. List all the ways Moses was commended for living "by faith" (verses 24-28).

Now look at each action and consider:

Why did it take faith to do it?

Whom or what did Moses place his faith in for each situation?

11. What happened to change Moses from the man at the burning bush to this man who lived to see God do all the incredible things listed here?

How does this encourage you?

FAITH INTO LIFE

Ephesians 2:10 tells us that we are "God's workmanship," created for his special calling and purposes for our lives. He not only gifts us, but he prepares us through the circumstances of our lives to accomplish those purposes. As you think of how God did this for Moses, consider again what God has placed in your hand. How has life shaped you? Will you believe in God enough to accept the assignments he gives you rather than dwelling on your own weaknesses? Remember, we don't serve God by being someone different from who we are. We serve him by trusting that he will use the unique person he created when he made us in Christ Jesus.

When Faith
Faces Death

EXODUS 13:17-22; 14; HEBREWS 11:29
(COMPLETE STORY: EXODUS 11–14)

Throughout life, in different ways, each of us faces moments when we must dare to risk some type of death before we are truly free to live. Such moments are never easy, whether we risk physical death or the death of some long-held dream, relationship, or comfort. Yet the Bible says that this is the ultimate law of life: Until we lose our lives, we will never find them. Without death—on whatever level—there can be no resurrection. Perhaps there are no greater moments of absolute faith than when we are asked to let go of all we hold dear without knowing what is on the other side.

This lesson looks at one such time for the children of Israel. They dared to leave behind the only world they had ever known—the familiar sights, sounds, and smells of Egypt. It may not have been perfect, but it was where they felt they belonged. Now they faced an incredible crossroads. Going ahead meant not only risking their physical lives but also losing the possibility of ever returning to life as they had known it. Turning back meant returning to what they knew, including slavery. What would they do?

1. Do you tend to play it safe in life situations, or do you venture out and take risks? Explain.

After Moses went back to Egypt and asked Pharaoh to let the Israelites go, Pharaoh initially refused, just as God had told Moses he would. God sent various plagues to convince Pharaoh that he must relent. After the last plague, when all the firstborn sons in the land were killed in one night, Pharaoh finally agreed to let the people go. See what happens next.

READ EXODUS 13:17-22.

2. What do you learn about God from verses 17 and 18?

What do you learn about the Israelites from these same verses?

∂ 3. How do we see Joseph's faith vindicated and Moses' faith revealed in verse 19?

∂ 4. Look at the means by which God led his people. Why do you think he chose to lead them this way?

Have you ever wished God would lead you in similar fashion? Explain.

READ EXODUS 14:1-31.

5. List the reasons God gave for his orders to Moses (verses 1-4).

✗ 6. Describe the next scene in verses 5-9. What did Pharaoh do? Why?

7. How did the Israelites react when the Egyptians pursued them (verses 10-12)?

How do you rate their faith in this situation? Why?

8. What was Moses' reply to the Israelites (verses 13-14)?

How do you rate his faith in this situation? Why?

9. Review what happened in verses 19-31.

What was God's role in making this happen?

What was Moses' role in making it happen?

What was the Israelites' role?

✒ 10. If any of these hadn't done their part, how would the story be different? Why is that important to think about?

Read Hebrews 11:29.

✐ 11.   Whose faith is commended in this verse?

Looking back to your answers for questions 7 and 8, how might you have passed out the "faith honors" for this occasion?

✐ 12.   When you consider what you've just read in Exodus, would you guess that the action that is commended was done primarily through faith or fear? Can both of these coexist? Explain.

Faith into Life

Despite the miraculous deliverance they experienced when they faced death by the Egyptians, the children of Israel later refused to trust God to deliver them when they faced enemies in the Promised Land. One faith victory does not ensure the next. Is it possible that, after giving your life to Jesus in the past, he now seems to be asking you to trust him in a new way, to "face death" and let go of even more? Perhaps you have never dared to let go and believe for the first time. Consider the reasons the Israelites could let go and trust God. Now consider your own situation. How will you respond?

When Faith Looks Up

HEBREWS 11:30–12:13

The stories of faith we have studied are different in their details but the same in one regard: All of the people in these stories looked beyond what they could see with their eyes to what they could not see—a loving God who was at work and in control. They made life-changing decisions to obey God's call and commands based on unseen realities. In the concluding verses of Hebrews 11, we see additional examples of the same faith, and in Hebrews 12 we learn more of how to respond in faith as we consider those who have gone before us.

1. Has doing this study made you more aware of God's working in your circumstances, both good and bad? Explain.

Read Hebrews 11:30-40.

2. List the outcomes for those who lived by faith as described in verses 30-35a.

3. What happened to others who also lived by faith (verses 35b-39)?

✣ 4. How do you reconcile these two outcomes?

What do these different outcomes say regarding the life of faith?

READ HEBREWS 12:1-13.

  ✐ 5. What does "therefore" in verse 1 refer us back to?

        Why do you think the writer of Hebrews wants us
        to remember what he has just written before we
        move on to his new instructions for us?

    6. What do the verbs used in verses 1 and 2 reveal about
       our faith walk?

  ✐ 7. What is the difference between "everything that
       hinders" us and "the sin that so easily entangles"
       us (verse 1)?

Why is it important to "throw off" both?

8. What does it mean that Jesus is "the author and perfecter of our faith" (verse 2)?

How does fixing our eyes on him help us walk by faith?

✍ 9. How would you define the kind of discipline described in verse 7? Is it the same as punishment? Explain.

10. What does God's discipline tell us about him? about ourselves?

11. How does this discipline relate to living by faith?

12. Reflect on verse 12, one more great "therefore." How do these words encourage you to move ahead and endure until the end in your own journey of faith?

FAITH INTO LIFE

As you complete this study on living by faith, reflect on what the people named in Hebrews 11 had in common in their faith journey. As you remember the many ways God worked in each of their lives to prepare them for his purposes, consider how he has worked in your life...through joy, through tears, through so many people and events. How have these various elements been part of God's discipline for you? Thank him that he is the same faithful God today that he was in ages past.

Leader's Notes

STUDY 1: WHAT IS FAITH?

Question 4. The writer of Hebrews is not known. While he didn't formally address the intended audience, the name and message of this book suggest he wrote it for Jewish Christians scattered abroad by persecution. Hebrews 10 shows that these Christians had endured early and severe persecution with joy and strong faith.

Question 7. Hebrews 11 doesn't say why Abel's sacrifice was better than Cain's or how it stemmed from faith. Looking back to Genesis 4, we see that God may have been pleased with Abel because he brought his very best, in contrast to only "some of the fruits" that his brother, Cain, gave. Maybe the commendation came because Abel offered an animal sacrifice rather than the produce Cain brought. (See Hebrews 9:22: "The law requires that nearly everything be cleansed with blood, and without the shedding of blood there is no forgiveness." Also, Hebrews 12:24 refers to the sacrifice of Jesus' blood being better than the blood of Abel.)

Question 9. Enoch had no listed pedigree, spectacular career, fancy title, or other tangible achievements by which we usually judge success. All we know is that Enoch walked so closely with God he never saw death. God obviously evaluates our lives by a different standard than what our world may use.

Question 10. Faith is not based on nebulous hope. Rather, it is rooted in the very character of God. All that God does and allows in our lives flows from One who is faithful, true, good, loving, kind, just, and more. Trusting in *who God is* when we can't understand what he is doing gives us hope in the midst of the most difficult circumstances. Trusting him is the key to living by faith rather than sight.

STUDY 2: WHEN FAITH MAKES YOU LOOK LIKE A FOOL

Question 3. Genealogies used in Scripture may or may not be exhaustive lists. They were used to pass down history orally from generation to generation (Adapted from *Life Application Bible,* Wheaton, Ill.: Tyndale, 1991, p. 16). Noah's lineage may give a clue as to why he could live as a righteous man in such an evil world. It may have been that the prayers and godly examples of those generations before him, including the stories he undoubtedly heard about his great-grandfather Enoch were part of Noah's spiritual formation. Our faith choices also affect those who come after us.

Question 4. God's reaction of sorrow and grief to the evil and violence he saw tells us much about his love for those he created as well as his view of sin.

Question 6. It is interesting to note that each time God gave instructions to Noah, there is no record of Noah's verbal reply. Instead, he demonstrated his faith in God and in what God said by unquestioningly obeying what God told him to do.

Question 10. Hebrews 11:7 tells us that Noah built the ark out of "holy fear" (reverence). "The Bible uses several words to denote fear. The most common of these are Heb. *yir'â,* 'reverence'; Heb. *pahad,* 'dread'; Gk. *phobos,* 'fear,' 'terror,'…a believer's apprehension of the living God" (*New Bible Dictionary,* Downers Grove, Ill.: InterVarsity, 1996, p. 365). Part of recognizing who God is includes knowing that he is not only a God of love but also a God who ultimately judges and punishes sin.

Question 11. Noah believed God would do what he said he would, so he took action on behalf of himself and his family, becoming an "heir of…righteousness." Just as God made a way for Noah to escape the watery judgment on the world, so through Jesus Christ, God has made a way for us to escape his coming judgment on our sins. Like Noah, we must act by faith to receive this gift.

STUDY 3: WHEN FAITH DOESN'T SEE THE PROMISE FULFILLED

Question 2. Abram's name was changed to *Abraham* later in Genesis 17:5.

Question 4. Genesis 11:27-28 says that Haran, the father of Lot and the brother of Abram, died. In many ancient cultures it was customary in such situations for the next oldest brother to adopt the dead relative's children into his own family. Lot may also have been Abram's backup plan as he contemplated how God might fulfill his promises, since Sarah had been barren up to that point (see Genesis 11:30).

Question 6. God told Abram his overall plan, but he didn't spell out every detail of how he would bring it about. Each reiteration and added clarification of the promise and the way it would be fulfilled came at a time when it would have been easy for Abram to give up. Often it is easy for us to confuse what God promises us with how and when we expect that promise to be fulfilled.

Question 8. While he undoubtedly didn't understand why God was asking him to sacrifice his son, Isaac, Abraham's faith led him to obedience—the ultimate mark of faith. After a lifetime of walking with God and seeing his faithfulness, Abraham knew that, even if Isaac died, God would still keep his promise.

STUDY 4: WHEN FAITH SEEMS ORDINARY

Question 3. Isaac would often have heard from his parents the story of his own miraculous conception and birth (see Genesis 17:15-21). Such a powerful story of how God gave him life must have helped him pray with confidence for God to intervene, even though his wife, Rebekah, had been infertile for twenty years.

Question 4. The law of that day said the *oldest* son should have a double portion of the father's property and that the younger son(s) would serve the older. With the reversal of this order in Genesis 25:23, God was preparing Isaac and Rebekah to accept his plan, not their's or the world's.

Question 6. Isaac had witnessed Abraham's faith and God's deliverance when Abraham placed him (Isaac) on the altar. But now Isaac was faced with his own crisis—there was no food for his people. It was in this moment that God encouraged him.

Question 7. Isaac exemplified faith by staying in the land despite the famine. Later, under God's equally clear permission and direction, Jacob went to Egypt for food (see Genesis 46:3). Living by faith means obeying what God says in each situation, not necessarily doing something the same way every time.

Question 9. The birthright of the eldest son was closely linked with the father's blessing of that son—a bestowal of good and often material wealth. In this particular case, the blessing included God's covenantal promises to Abraham and Isaac and their descendants.

Question 11. Isaac's life depicts one of the harder places of faith: enduring and obeying in the long haul of the ordinary things of life. Through Isaac's day-by-day obedience, God was establishing the beginnings of the new nation he promised to form.

Study 5: When Faith Seems Absent

Question 2. The mystery of God's grace is clearly seen in this vignette. During a time when Jacob was demonstrating anything but faith, God appeared to him while he slept—a completely "unseeking" state!

Question 3. God made the same promises to Jacob that he had given to Abraham and Isaac (see Genesis 12:2; 15:18; 26:3), thereby defining Jacob as the person through whom these covenantal promises would be fulfilled. It is amazing that in his fearful, sinful condition, Jacob was called by God for such eternal purposes. Again, a story of God's grace.

Question 5. After marrying Rachel, Jacob traveled back to his homeland, passing through the area where Esau, the brother he had cheated, lived. The angels were like those he saw in his dream at Bethel during his initial flight from Esau's wrath. Through them, God gave Jacob another opportunity to reflect on his long-ago promises and to trust that God would not fail him now.

Question 8. In this wonderful picture we see images of our own stories. In renaming Jacob, God focused on who he called Jacob *to be* rather than on who or what Jacob had been. This is a foretaste of the truth in 2 Corinthians 5:17: "If anyone is in Christ, he is a new creation." Also, Revelation 2:17 and 3:12 say that one day God will give us each a new name.

Question 12. Read Genesis 48 for the full account of Jacob's blessing of Joseph's sons. In the blessing he specifically passed on the covenantal promises of God, thereby expressing his faith that God would do as he said in every detail, even though he (Jacob) had not yet seen it happen.

STUDY 6: WHEN FAITH TRUSTS ENOUGH TO FORGIVE

Question 2. Here we see Jacob repeating the patterns of favoritism that so devastated the family in which he grew up (see Genesis 27). The bad news is that he didn't seem to learn from the past. The good news is that God's will and plan were still being accomplished despite human sin and frailties.

Question 5. "Tearing one's clothes and wearing sackcloth were signs of mourning, much like wearing black today" (*Life Application Bible,* p. 78).

Question 7. For a full account of the intervening years and how Joseph became second in command in the land of Egypt, read Genesis 39–44.

Question 8. In spite of the fact that what his brothers did was wrong, Joseph recognized that God had prepared him through each circumstance of his life, including his brothers' betrayal, to be the man God would use to save his own people. Romans 8:28 reminds us that we, too, can rejoice because our Redeemer God can turn any situation in our lives to good, as he did for Joseph.

Question 12. Joseph remained convinced that God would not fail in keeping his promises to give the Israelites a land of their own, and he wanted to be buried in that land. The Israelites carried out his request by taking his bones with them in their exodus out of Egypt (Exodus 13:19) and later burying them in Canaan (Joshua 24:32).

STUDY 7: WHEN FAITH RECEIVES AN IMPOSSIBLE CALL

Question 2. If background is needed, read Exodus 1–2 to see where we pick up Moses' story for this lesson. Acts 7:17-44 also gives an excellent overview of Moses' life.

Question 3. It's interesting to note that God identified himself as the covenantal God, "the God of your father, the God of Abraham, the God of Isaac and the God of Jacob" (Exodus 3:6). He also included Moses in the covenant, "I am the God of *your* father..." (verse 6, emphasis added), an amazing reality for one who had grown up in the palace of Pharaoh, away from the Jewish environment.

Question 4. Moses was well acquainted with the suffering of his people from his years of growing up in Egypt in Pharaoh's household (see Exodus 2:11-15). It was because Moses killed a man while trying to help his people that he was in exile in Midian. Now God would do what Moses had been unable to do.

Question 9. In the end, Moses obeyed in spite of his doubts. "Lord, I believe; help my unbelief!" (Mark 9:24, NKJV) also expresses legitimate faith. We also see God as a person who is willing to come to wherever we are in the journey to grow us up when we can't quite believe enough to make a total faith leap to him. As someone once said, "God takes us as we are, not as we should be."

STUDY 8: WHEN FAITH FACES DEATH

Question 3. Four hundred years after Joseph's request (Genesis 50:22-26), his bones were now being taken by Moses as the people left Egypt. Without faith, Joseph wouldn't have asked to be taken to the Promised Land. Without faith that the people would reach it, Moses would have had no reason to carry the extra "luggage" of Joseph's bones on this difficult journey through an unknown wilderness.

Question 4. The visible cloud and fiery pillar bore witness for all to see that God himself was leading them rather than Moses alone. This was God's way of giving clear guidance to each person. The Israelites needed to know that crossing the Red Sea was God's plan rather than a human one, or no one would have dared to try.

Question 6. Sometimes it's difficult to accept that God ordains events that don't seem "good" to us. Yet the Bible tells us that God holds the king's heart in his hands (Proverbs 21:1). We cannot deny that God himself hardened Pharaoh's heart and set events in motion. Those times when we can't understand what is happening are the times we must have faith in the very character of God, not in our own expectations of what he will do.

Question 10. At times it's easy to think that what we do doesn't matter in the bigger scheme of things. If God and Moses had done their parts in dividing the waters, but no one had dared to walk across, the Israelites would not have experienced God's salvation.

Question 11. Here we see the power and importance of corporate as well as individual faith.

Question 12. Sometimes faith is obeying in spite of how we feel. Despite their fears and groanings beforehand, when the moment came to cross the Red Sea, the people took the steps to move into and through the parted waters. Their actions were counted as faith regardless of their feelings.

STUDY 9: WHEN FAITH LOOKS UP

Question 4. The outcome is not what defines living "by faith." God sees things from a very different perspective than we often do. It is easy to presume that walking by faith means a happy ending, that God will do everything we desire. By comparing these stories with radically different outcomes, we see how God values the process of faith and obedience, not just the specific results.

Question 5. Anytime you see a *therefore* in Scripture, look to see what it's *there for*.

Question 7. Scripture makes it clear that some actions and behaviors go against God's laws and are thus sin. There is no question that we are to "throw off" these behaviors. But each of us also has customs or habits or pleasures that are not clearly defined in Scripture as sin. Yet they may take our time and attention from eternal things to such a degree that they side-track us from running a solid spiritual race. These hindrances can be harder to let go of than sins because they are so easy to justify.

Question 9. Merriam Webster's Collegiate Dictionary says that *punishment* is "to inflict a penalty on someone for wrong-doing." It is always associated with wrong or sinful behavior. Discipline, while sometimes a punishment for bad or sinful behavior, is a much larger concept. It also includes "training that corrects, molds, or perfects the mental faculties or moral character." In Hebrews 12, the discipline of God is likened to that of a good father. Whatever he does to correct or train us is always and only for our ultimate good and his glory, never for our harm.

The Fisherman Bible Studyguide Series—
Get Hooked on Studying God's Word

Old Testament Studies

Genesis

Proverbs

Acts 1-12

Acts 13-28

Colossians

James

New Testament Studies

Mark

John

Romans

Philippians

1, 2, 3 John

Revelation

Women of the Word

Becoming Women
of Purpose

Wisdom for
Today's Woman

Women Like Us

Women Who
Believed God

For more information, visit our Web site: www.waterbrookmultnomah.com

Topical Studies

Building Your
House on the Lord

Discipleship

Encouraging
Others

The Fruit of the
Spirit

Growing Through
Life's Challenges

Guidance and
God's Will

Higher Ground

Lifestyle Priorities

The Parables of
Jesus

Parenting with
Purpose and Grace

Prayer

Proverbs &
Parables

The Sermon on
the Mount

Speaking Wisely

Spiritual
Disciplines

Spiritual Gifts

Spiritual Warfare

The Ten
Commandments

When Faith Is
All You Have

Who Is the
Holy Spirit?